A Parenting Press Qwik Book

Children and Chores

The **Surprising Impact of Chores on Kids' Fut**

Elizabeth Crary

Parenting Press
Chicago

Contents

■ **CHAPTER ONE: Why bother with chores? 4**
Research • What is a chore? • Why chores are powerful • Notes
on research • A chore by any other name • Now is the time to
begin

■ **CHAPTER TWO: What can I expect of my child? 7**
Developmental stage • Temperament • Interest, experience, and
aversions • Learning styles • Chore ideas for different ages

■ **CHAPTER THREE: How to teach chores 12**
Make the job clear • Offer choices (limited) • Create a reminder
system • Give support • Establish consequences • Make a plan

■ **CHAPTER FOUR: Dealing with resistence 22**
Forgets the chore • Poor quality work • Refusal to contribute

■ **CHAPTER FIVE: Tie chores to allowances? 26**
Purpose of allowances • Impact of money on chores • A balanced
approach

■ **CHAPTER SIX: Changing as kids grow 28**
Levels of support • Vary the jobs • Growing a chore as the child
grows

■ **CLOSING 31**

■ **RESOURCES 32**

Copyright © 2011 by Elizabeth Crary

ISBN 978-1-884734-92-2
www.ParentingPress.com

PARENTING PRESS, INC.
814 North Franklin Street
Chicago, Illinois 60610

Welcome!

You are probably reading this book because you are curious what impact chores can have on kids' futures or you want to involve kids in chores and don't know how.

Children and Chores: The Surprising Impact of Chores on Kids' Futures was written to—
- Explain why chores are so important
- Clarify what you can expect from children at different ages
- Offer a process to introduce kids to chores
- Share strategies for dealing with resistence
- Illustrate how to change chores as your child grows

If these topics are of interest, then this book is for you.

The key to involving kids with chores is having realistic expectations, a clear process, and lots of persistent patience.

Have fun with these ideas and tools.

—Elizabeth Crary

CHAPTER 1

Why bother with chores?

Starting chores early encourages responsibility, self-care know-how, and self-discipline in young adults.

Research

Marty Rossmann (University of Minnesota) has found that involving children in household tasks beginning at age three or four is the single best predictor of success in young adulthood.

Criteria for success. Rossmann looked at what the young adults were doing. Success meant they were finished with their education or on track for completion, they had some clear career path, their relationships with family and friends were positive, and they were not using drugs.

Chores are more important than parenting styles, students' IQ or gender, the types of household tasks expected, and the attitudes and motivators used to encourage doing the tasks. This was surprising since conventional wisdom holds that IQ and motivation have a strong bearing on success, but Rossmann found that these don't matter nearly as much as participating in household tasks.

How the tasks were presented also made a difference. In order for chores to have a positive impact they need to be presented in a kind and consistent way, Rossmann found. Each task was—
  • age appropriate and not overwhelming to the young child,
  • mastered before another one was added, and
  • explained in the child's learning style (auditory, visual, kinesthetic).
Further, the child was permitted a choice in tasks, and chores were not connected to an allowance. Rossmann's research shows the powerful results from involving young children in household chores.

Lack of childhood chores often causes pain in adulthood. Jean Illsley Clarke, in *How Much Is Enough?*, points out from her research that adults who were overindulged by not having to do household chores experience pain in adulthood due to lack of skills, low self-esteem, and a sense of entitlement.

What is a chore?

A *chore* is a routine task or job. Once it is learned, a person is expected to do his or her chores in a timely fashion without prompting. Chores are an ongoing way of contributing to the family. *"My job is to set the table before dinner."*

A *directive*, on the other hand, is a statement expecting action. A person is usually expected to comply fairly quickly. *"Set the table,"* or *"Set the table, now."*

Q What is the difference among a *request*, a *directive*, and a *chore*?

A *request* is a statement asking for something. Because it asks, it implies that a person may choose to comply or not. It is generally characterized by courteous phrasing like, *"Will you set the table?" "Please set the table,"* or *"I'd like you to set the table."*

Why chores are powerful

Chores are influential not only for the household skills kids learn, but also for the self-management lessons children learn as they strive to do their chores and what they wish to do. Some specific skills are described below.

- *Home management skills/know-how.* Kids learn to do many household tasks, among them clean, cook, do laundry, vacuum, shop and in some families, manage the budget.
- *Reciprocal nature of life.* Children who do chores learn to give to the family as well as receive from the family.
- *Self-esteem.* By doing chores children realize they have a role or function in their family. They develop a sense of importance without entitlement.
- *Self-motivation.* Most chores become routine after a while. Kids learn how to do a job (task) regardless of whether it is enjoyable.
- *Prioritizing activities.* If kids are going to do what they want to do and their chores, they must plan their time so they get done what is most important.
- *Self-confidence.* The child learns he can take care of himself.
- *Project management.* As kids grow older and chores become more complex, they learn to define the task, learn skills, DO IT, and tidy up after. These steps are an integral part of project management.

Notes on research

- **Chores are powerful.** Professor Rossmann's research shows that the earlier you start, the sooner the values of giving to the family, following through with commitments, and self-discipline are incorporated into your child. Also, the earlier you involve children in the household tasks, the easier it will be to involve them as teens.
- **No guarantee.** Requiring kids to do chores does not guarantee that they will be successful in their mid-twenties. There are many life experiences that can interfere, but it does significantly increase the odds of success.
- **Multiple paths to success.** Similarly, starting routine chores late or not at all does not prevent the children from doing well as young adults. Although Rossmann's research looked at several factors it did not look at all life experience. I believe the elements that chores provide (giving to the family or community, following through with commitments, and developing self-discipline) can be learned in other ways, particularly if the parents require personal responsibility and avoid overnurturing their children (doing things for them that they are developmentally capable of).

A chore by any other name . . .

The word "chore" is loaded with unpleasant associations for many people—You must, . . . It will be unpleasant, . . . I will force you to. . . . Many families have had success by changing the focus to "helping." You might say, "In our family we help each other. Babies are so helpless we have to help them with almost everything. When they get bigger they can begin to help. You're already big enough. Here are things we need to do today. Which task do you want to help with first?"

Now is the time to begin

Next, we will look at what you can expect of your child. Whether your child is a preschooler or school-aged, there is no time like the present to begin.

Life would be easier for parents if all children could do the same tasks at the same time. That way you could look at a chart of chores and ages to determine what is reasonable. Life is not that simple. The ability to do a task is influenced by four factors: the child's developmental stage, temperament, interest and experience, and learning style.

Developmental stage

Unfortunately, young children are interested in doing household tasks before they have the ability to work independently. Then they have the ability to do a task before they have the emotional maturity to complete the task alone.

Children go through three stages on the way to independent competence:
- Child helps with the chore. Parent does the planning and provides motivation, and the child does part of the work.
- Child needs reminding or supervision. The adult and child share planning, motivation, and work.
- Child completes the task alone most of the time. The child does the planning, motivation, and work (including clean-up).

The reminding stage can be deceiving because a child can often do the task with no difficulty when the parent is present. However, the child cannot sustain the focus when the parent leaves nor can he work alone the next time. There is a difference in the ability to do a task alone and the ability to be responsible for doing the task alone.

The process is illustrated in Figure 1: Household jobs readiness. You can see that it often takes kids years, rather than weeks or months, to move from one stage to the next. Another way to see this change is in Chart 1, which shows how the task of cleaning the bathroom can change as the child grows.

Figure 1: Household jobs readiness

Task	Ages and Involvement										
	3	4	5	6	7	8	9	10	11	12	13
Pick up stuff	H------------------------------R------------------------A										
Make bed	H-------------------------------------R--------A										
Tidy room	H----------------------------------R-------------A										
Wipe spills	H---------------------------------R-----A										
Care for pet	H---------------------------------R--------A										
Set table	H---R----A										
	3	4	5	6	7	8	9	10	11	12	13

H = needs help   R = needs reminding   A = is able and independent

Chart 1: How a chore can grow with a child

Bathroom items to be cleaned	Toddler 1-3 yrs	Preschooler 3-6 yrs	Elementary school 6-8 yrs	Elementary school 9-11 yrs
Mirror, sink & counter • Spray and wipe with no streaks • Remove grit and toothpaste globs	helps you	with help	alone	alone
Toilet • Outside–wipe off top to bottom • Lid & seat–spray and wipe • Bowl–spray and scrub with brush	helps you	with help	coaching or alone	alone
Tub/shower • Spray and wipe tub or stall • Check for streaks/grit. Re-do if found	helps you	with help	w/help or coaching	coaching or alone
Windows • Spray and wipe; check for streaks	helps you	w/help or coaching	alone	alone
Towels, toilet paper, trash • Put clean towels on the rack • Get toilet paper if needed • Get bag and dump out garbage	with help	w/help or coaching	alone	alone
Floors • Sweep or vacuum • Mop floor with cleaner and dry	helps you	w/help or coaching	w/help or coaching	coaching or alone

General observations

- *Toddlers.* (0-2 years) Many toddlers want to help, but their "help" may not be useful. Keep their interest alive by involving them where you can—you are establishing the habit of cooperation and laying the groundwork for feeling good about helping out.

- *Preschoolers* (3-5 years) often find learning new chores interesting when they are clearly explained. You can use this interest to create a routine.
- *School-aged kids* (6-8 years) may outgrow their interest in chores, and want to be independent. Sometimes this desire to be independent can be used to involve kids in chores. School-aged kids usually need reminding (see Figure 1).
- *Pre-teens* (9-12 years) are capable of more responsibility, but are often resistant to chores if they have not been involved at an early age. For chores to be a success, pre-teens need a clear structure. Find a system that works for your family and change it only with input from all directly affected.

Temperament

Temperament is the set of inborn traits that affect how a child views the world. These traits influence how comfortable a child is learning new things and how long he will persist if learning is difficult.

Ten temperament traits are listed in the sidebar. Each trait can range from high (intense) to low (weak or mild).

When you choose a task for your child you may want to consider her traits. The following are several ways temperament traits might influence what chore you decide to introduce to her.

Temperament Traits

Activity level
Adaptability
Approach
   (curious/cautious)
Distractibility
Emotional sensitivity
Intensity
Mood
Persistence
Physical sensitivity
Regularity

- *Children with high activity levels* can channel that energy into more active chores like sweeping, scrubbing, or raking leaves.
- *Both highly distractible and low persistence* children need to be taught how to focus on a task. Praise and rewards often help.
- *Kids with a high physical sensitivity to smell* may be overwhelmed by a stinky task or cleaning chemicals. A child with acute hearing may not like noisy vacuum cleaners.
- *Children who are cautious (low approach)* may need more explanation of what to expect.

If you would like more information about temperament, check the resources list on page 32.

Interest, experience, and aversions

Some children have strong feelings that influence their willingness to do specific chores.

Interests. Here are three stories of how families responded to their child's interests.

Jack (age 2¾) wanted to vacuum. Dad had an infinite store of patience. He set about to teach Jack how to vacuum. After nine months of teaching and supervising, Dad had a 3½-year-old who vacuumed the carpets and wooden floors.

Janie loved animals. Instead of setting the table she would play with the cats. Her mom taught her to feed the cats and scoop their litter box.

Adam had the job of emptying all the trash baskets each Saturday. He was tired of doing it. His parents wrote all the family chores on slips of paper and asked him to select another chore. He decided to trade emptying trash for a chore that was more interesting to him.

Experiences. Skills learned in one area are often transferable to another. If a child can put away toys in her own room, she may be able to help a younger child in another room.

Ellie (age 10) went to a cooking camp with her best friend. When she came home, she was excited to show her family all the things she had leaned to cook. Her mom let her trade her previous chore for fixing breakfast for the whole family each Saturday morning.

Aversions. Sometimes there are reasons for the aversion, sometimes not. Children bothered by smells may dislike taking out the kitchen compost. Sometimes teenage boys don't like to wash dishes.

If the dislike is very strong, there are two approaches. One is to let the child substitute an equivalent task. Second is to tell the child that when he demonstrates that he can do the chore well, he can select another chore to replace it.

Learning styles

A learning style is how a person collects information, or his or her preferred way of learning. Three common learning styles are visual, auditory, and kinesthetic/tactile.

Visual learning style. Children use their eyes to learn. They prefer what they can see, such as objects, movement, or color. They would rather look than listen.

Auditory learning style. Auditory children like to listen and talk. They remember both the words and the tune of songs easily.

Kinesthetic learning style. Kinesthetic children like to learn by touching and moving. They often like to take things apart.

Learning styles affect how you will need to present information to your child. For example, a visual child might prefer to look at a diagram of where to put things on the table when setting it. An auditory learner would prefer someone to tell her where things go. A kinesthetic child might prefer to start putting things on the table and receive explanation as he goes along.

Similarly, when reminders are needed, a visual child would usually prefer a note or picture, an auditory child a verbal reminder, and a kinesthetic child a gentle hand on her shoulder.

Chore ideas for different ages

As children grow they are capable of doing more complex tasks. Some tasks may need clarifying or training regardless of how old the child is. Elements to consider when introducing a chore are presented in the next chapter, *"How to teach chores."*

There are two approaches to deciding what chores are reasonable for your child.

- **The _chore-based_ approach:** Look at a chore and plan how you would introduce it, depending on your child's age and other traits. (See chart 1, p. 8.)
- **The _child-based_ approach:** Consider your child's age and check the chart below (see chart 2, p. 12) to see what chores are appropriate for that age.

When you look at the chore ideas list remember that many chores assume some prior knowledge. When children lack some prerequisite skills, they will need to learn them before they can do tasks listed for their age.

11

Now that we have looked at what is reasonable to expect for different children we will look at how to start or teach a new chore.

Chart 2: Chore ideas for children of different ages			
Ages 2-3	**Ages 4-5**	**Ages 6-8**	**Ages 9-12**
Help feed pets	*earlier tasks plus*	*earlier tasks plus*	*earlier tasks plus*
Help wipe up messes	Let pet in and out	Feed and water pets	Clean kitchen
Shred lettuce for salad	Set the table	Empty the dishwasher	counters & sink
Help mix ingredients	Help clear non-	Put away clean dry	Load the dishwasher
Help make the bed	breakables from	dishes	Prepare simple meals
Help pick up toys and	the table	Fix a snack	Pack own lunch
books	Help prepare food	Pick up their belong-	Make bed
Put dirty clothes	Put shoes away	ings	Tidy room with
in hamper when	Put forks and spoons	Fold and put away	reminding
asked	away	laundry	Operate washer and
Do simple errands,	Pull bed covers up	Take out trash	dryer
"Bring the diaper,	Put their clean clothes	Help vacuum	Fold and put away
please" "Throw	in the drawer	Clean inside of the car	laundry
this in the trash,	Wipe the bathroom	Water the garden	Clean mirrors
please"	sink	Help rake leaves	Clean the bathroom
	Water indoor plants		Help wash the car
			Rake leaves

CHAPTER 3: **How to Teach Chores**

Here are five elements to include when you involve your kids in chores. At the end of each element is a box where you can apply the concept just presented to a task of your choice. Once you have thought through these elements you can make a plan to teach a chore.

1. Make the job clear

It is easier to do a good job if the child knows what is expected.

Determine what is reasonable for the child's age. Consider age, temperament, and experience. We looked at this in the previous chapter.

Get the child's attention. This may sound obvious, but some parents start talking before checking to see that the child is listening. Get eye level with the child. Consider the child's learning style: show a visual child what to do, tell an auditory child, and do it with a kinesthetic child.

Explain what is included in the chore. Describe how much is enough and what is excellent.

For example, "Clean your room" might mean: floor is clear, dirty clothes are in the hamper, toys/books are on a shelf, and the bedspread is pulled up. Or it might also include floor swept or vacuumed, toys organized on the shelf, and books alphabetized.

Does "Pick up your toys in the living room and put them away," mean pick up books and clothes, too? What about a sibling's toys? Clarify exactly what you mean.

Establish a deadline. With older kids a time deadline is fine. "Put the dishes away before 5 P.M. so I can cook dinner." "Take the trash out before 8 P.M." With young children tie the deadline to an event. For example, "Pick up your toys": a) "so we can go to the park," b) "before lunch," c) "before Daddy comes home to surprise him" or d) "immediately after dinner."

■ **Make the job clear.**

Think of a task and write exactly what you want:

- task _____
- deadline _____
- standard _____

---

2. Offer choices (limited)

Children are more likely to participate if they feel they have some input in the decision. If the job feels overwhelming, they won't start. You can offer a child help or no help, choice of deadline (date or time), which task of several, the tools he or she might use, or the order in which to do things. Examples:

- "Do you want to empty the trash or set the table?"
- "Would you prefer to clean alone or do you want me to help?"
- "Do you want to pick two chores to do this month or do you want me to assign them?"
- "Would you like me to pick up the books or the blocks?"

■ **What choices can I offer for the task I chose?**

"You can _____

or _____."

13

3. Create a reminder system

Two kinds of reminders are useful—a reminder to do the task, and a reminder to do the *whole* task.

Reminder to DO the task. Starting a new habit is hard for many people (grown-ups and children). It helps to have a reminder system until the new behavior (chore) becomes a habit. Below is a list of things that have worked for some people.

- *Timer*—set to put away toys or set the table
- *Calendar*—note which sibling sets the table and which cleans up after supper
- *Reminder song*—"Time to put toys away," or "Clean up, clean up, everybody helps clean up."

> **Clean-up song**
> It's time to put the *toys* away, *toys* away, *toys* away,
> It's time to put the *toys* away so we can go *outside*.
>
> Note: Words in *italic* can be changed as desired.

- *Poster*—prominently displayed on the child's door picturing a clean room.
- *Flicking the lights*—in the room where the child is when it is time to do the chore.
- *Tie a string* around a finger or put a watch on the "wrong" arm—something that feels odd and calls attention to itself. When the item is noticed the child is reminded to do the task.
- *Place a chair in the path.* For example, if you want your son to feed the dog before playing in his room or watching TV, place a chair in the doorway to his room (or in front of the TV) with a picture of a dog on it.
- *Leave a message* on the child's cell phone, or better yet, ask the child to leave herself a message.

Reminder to do ALL of the task. Many children start a chore but don't finish it. One reason is that they forget all that is involved. Here are some ideas that might help.

- *Help cards.* File cards with pictures of the items needed to set the table (placemat, napkin, glass, plate, knife, fork, and spoon). The cards might also include a picture of where they go. Even children who cannot read can follow the pictures and do the chore.

- *Five-finger check*. Each finger represents one part of the task that is to be done.

- *Checklist for the task.* Some children, particularly those who like computers or art work, like to make checklists and decorate them.

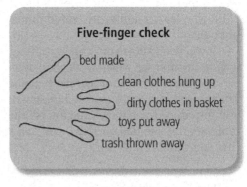

Five-finger check

bed made
clean clothes hung up
dirty clothes in basket
toys put away
trash thrown away

- *Make a story board* or comic strip. Story board is similar to the help cards, however, the steps in the story board are fixed in sequence.

- *Invent a song or chant.* In the side bar is a song that can be modified to fit the situation.

Clean ALL Your Room
(To *Row, row, row your boat*)

Clean, clean ALL your room,
Put your toys away.
Hang up your clothes
And make your bed.
Do it every day.

Clean, clean ALL your room,
Put your books away.
Pick up your trash
And sweep the floor.
Then you get to play!

Which system should I use? The goal is to choose a system that will help the child. Often parents create a reminder that appeals to them rather than to their child. To increase the odds of success, you can chose a reminder system that supports your child's learning style or simply ask the child what might work for him.

Try the child's learning style. There are three general learning styles: kinesthetic (movement), auditory/verbal, and visual. The examples above provide ideas for each learning style. For example, a child who learns by moving may prefer the help cards, while a child who is more visual usually prefers the story board or comic strip. A child who learns auditorily would probably like the reminder song or chant.

If you don't know your child's learning style you can try all three approaches and see which works best or ask your child what might help.

Ask the child what might work. Some children, particularly school aged, are more invested in something they help set up. When you introduce the chore, you can ask the child what would help her remember. If she has no ideas, you can suggest several approaches that you think might work.

Possible reminder systems
What do you think your child's learning style is? _____

_____

What are two reminder systems that might work:
- _____
- _____

4. Give support

You can give support by rewarding desired behavior, making the chore fun, and letting the child ask for help.

Model making chores fun. One challenge in life is learning how to enjoy what you must do. A playful, curious attitude is helpful.
- *Work with the child.* Children aren't designed to work alone. Most children, particularly young ones, want to be with people. When they are forced to work alone they get distracted and the task becomes drudgery.
- *Pretend someone fun is coming* and you are getting ready. It could be a dinosaur king, cartoon characters, fairy princess, favorite aunt or uncle—someone the child likes and admires.
- *Be silly.* Use tongs or mittens to put things away. Pick up toys with your toes. Walk backwards. It may slow things down but makes them fun.
- *Use a story character.* Pretend to be Cinderella, Laura from *Little House on the Prairie,* or Tom Sawyer doing their chores.

Scrub the hearth could become mop the kitchen, bring in the eggs could be put the groceries away, or paint the fence could be wash the car.

- *Make a game.* Find everything with an A (animals) and put them away, then B (books, blocks), and so on. Put a basketball hoop over a clothes hamper and let the child make "baskets" with his or her dirty clothes.
- *Turn on lively music.* Music can make work more fun.
- *Roll a chore.* The die can be used to choose a chore (even numbers mean set the table; odd numbers, clear the table) or where to start a task (1 = make bed, 2 = dirty clothes in the hamper, 3 = toys on the shelf, 4 = trash in the wastepaper basket, 5 = backpack by the door, 6 = roll again).
- *Beat your record.* Try to clean your room faster than last time.

Possible ways to make the task fun

- You can _____
- Or _____.

Permit the child to ask for help. Children go through three stages in learning to do a task: they help, they need reminding, and finally they do it alone.

For some reason, giving kids permission to ask for help often enables them to work independently. I explain this to myself by noticing that when I am learning a new software program I am fine as long as the person teaching me is near. However, when she leaves, I often have difficulty remembering what I could do only a few minutes ago. You can say, "Ask me if you need help," or "Tell me what part you need help with."

Encourage desired behavior. Children are more likely to continue doing a chore when you acknowledge their effort. You can use attention, praise, or rewards.

- *Attention.* Attention can be a smile, a high five, or simply being near your child. Attention is a powerful motivator and may explain why helping children do a task works so well.
- *Praise.* Comment on the behavior you like. Praise can be descriptive, appreciative, or evaluative. Descriptive praise might be, "You put all the toys away. The trucks, blocks, books, and puzzles are all on the shelf where they belong." Appreciative praise might be, "Thank you for putting the

17

toys away. The room looks neat and clean now." Evaluative praise might be, "You did a good job. Everything is where it belongs."

- **Rewards.** The goal of rewards is to help your child build a new habit. Rewards must be something the child needs or wants. They can be immediate or delayed. Immediate might be, "As soon as your toys are picked up we can have lunch." Or, "When the dishwasher is empty I will play a game with you." Delayed rewards might be accumulating tokens or tickets for an activity or privilege. An activity might be a trip to the ball game, visit to the zoo, or baking cookies. A privilege might be a later bedtime one night, a friend overnight, or extra screen time. You can find more information about encouraging desired behavior in the resources section.

Reward <u>responsibility</u> more than <u>obedience</u>. If you want your child to do chores independently without reminding, then it is helpful to reward the independence more than compliance. For example, if you offer your child one sticker for picking up her toys when reminded, give her two for picking them up without reminding. If you give your son one token for taking the trash out each evening when reminded, give him two tokens for doing it before you remind him.

Ways to acknowledge my child's contribution

- Parents can _____
- Or _____

5. Establish consequences

Clarify consequences before a child slips up. Use only consequences you will follow through with consistently. If your children leave their toys around in spite of your reminders, decide what you will do. Don't say you will throw their toys away unless you actually will. Instead, you might say you will make them disappear for a week.

Ask older children to predict your response. For example, "What do you think will happen if the timer rings and your room is still messy?" or "What will I answer if you ask to have a friend overnight and your room is not clean?" In this way you are *helping the children* consider the consequence of their actions rather than expecting them to listen to you yet again.

Possible consequences

- Parent can _____

- Or _____

Make a plan

Decide on the chore. Consider your child's age, temperament, and experience and interest, and decide what chore you wish her to help with. For example, suppose you want your child to help set the table. If your child is very young you might not want her to carry breakable glasses or plates. Also, if the child is small she might not be able to reach the table easily. So, ask yourself, is this chore reasonable for my child, or can I modify it so that it is?

Decide how to teach.
- *List the steps and decide their order.* Most tasks involve several steps. Often we are so used to doing the chore that we are unaware of the different parts. For example, there are four general steps involved in setting the table. You can see these in the sidebar.

Setting the table
1. Get out items needed: placemats, plates, knives, forks, spoons, glasses, and napkins.
2. Put the placemats on the table.
3. Put a plate, silverware, glass, and napkin at each place.
4. Check that items are in the proper place.

- *Choose where to begin.* Sometimes it is easier to start your child with the first step, sometimes with the last step. For example, if you want to teach your son to put on his shirt, you can start by putting it almost all on and letting him finish putting the final arm in. Or, you could position the shirt over his head, let him pull it down, and then you could finish putting his arms in and pulling the shirt down.

19

- *Plan to engage cooperation.* For ideas, refer to the section "Give support" on pages 16–18.

Schedule a time to evaluate progress. With luck, your plan will work; often, however, plans need to be tweaked. Decide how long you will try the plan before reviewing it. When you evaluate consider what went well and what needs to change.

Congratulate yourself. When you have completed your plan and evaluated it acknowledge your effort. You put effort in and deserve recognition. Since your child is unlikely to say, "Thanks, Mom [Dad]. I know I will appreciate this when I am an adult," you can say it for yourself.

You can see how this process works in the following example.

Chart 3: Plan for setting the table	
The step	**The example**
Background Child's name and age Chore I would like done	Gracie, age 4½ Set the table for supper
Decide how to teach List the steps involved	See sidebar, "Setting the Table" for the order of steps
Choose where to begin	I will put placemats and plates on. Then I'll give Gracie all the items for one placemat. When she's done I'll give her stuff for the next.
Plan to engage cooperation	Gracie loves craft projects. I will ask her to help me make placemats that have the positions of different items marked.
Introducing the chore Make the job clear	To put items at the places each night for dinner. I will get things out for her.
Offer choices (limited)	"Do you want to go around the table to the right or to the left?"
Create reminder system	Set a timer for ten and five minutes before dinner.
Give support or reward	I will be with her while she works. If she comes before the first buzz, she may choose the color of napkins for dinner.
Establish consequences	If she "forgets" she will reimburse me for the time it took to do her job—either help me load the dishwasher or miss her evening stories.
Do It	
Evaluate progress Date to review	I'll review the plan in both three days and a week.
What went well? What needs to change?	She was excited about setting the table. In three days it was obvious I needed to allow twice as much time. She was amazingly slow.
Congratulate yourself	I did good! My plan worked well with a little tweaking.

Your plan	
Background	
Child's name and age	
Chore I would like done	
Decide how to teach	
List the steps involved	
Choose where to begin	
Plan to engage cooperation	
Introducing the chore	
Make the job clear	
Offer choices (limited)	
Create reminder system	
Give support or reward	
Establish consequences	
Do It	
Evaluate progress	
Date to review	
What went well?	
What needs to change?	
Congratulate yourself	
How will you reward yourself?	

CHAPTER **4**: **Dealing with resistence**

Some children can't be bothered to interrupt themselves to do a chore and others actively resist.

Forgets the chore

Many children are easily distracted—it is one of the temperament traits. You need to help these children build strategies to remember a task until the chore becomes a habit. Professionals specializing in helping people make change say that it takes at least 21 days to build a new habit.

During the first several days or first week of a new chore, the child may remember consistently, however, when the initial excitement wears off many children get distracted or lose interest. This is when a reminder system is very helpful, particularly when coupled with encouragement and/or consequences.

Reminder systems. Ideally, you want your child to remember and act independently. The most effective reminder is one that does not involve you; if that is not possible, then asking the child what will help him remember may work. Be sensitive to learning style.

- *Self-announcing reminders.* With these reminders, something about the chore itself brings the task to mind. For example, Brian is to walk the dog after school. When Brian gets home, the dog enthusiastically greets Brian and may, depending on the dog, actually bring Brian the leash.

  If a preschool child is supposed to set his place for lunch, hunger will eventually drive the child to put his dishes on the table. These are nice reminders because they do not involve you directly. The main challenge for the parent is resisting the temptation to remind the child.

- *Learning style–compatible reminder.* Often, wishing to be helpful, parents will make a reminder system that works well for the parent. If the child's learning style is the same as the parent's, that may work. However, if the learning style is different, the reminder system may not work regardless of how appealing it is to the parent.

  Look at the list of reminders to do a task (page 14) and decide which reminder works with each learning style. Some

22

ideas are listed in the box at the right.

- *Rotate jobs or permit the child to choose the chores of the week.* Some kids "forget" because the task is boring. For these kids, it is easier to remember and do tasks when the chores vary day-to-day or week-to-week.
- *Let the child create his or her own reminder system.* When children create their own reminder systems, it usually works better because they are more invested in them. They may draw a poster to remind them how to clean the kitchen, or set their cell phone to remind them to take out the trash after dinner.

Learning style and reminders

Visual:	Timer (if large dial), calendar, poster, flicking the lights
Auditory:	Timer (if rings), reminder song, message on child's cell phone
Kinesthetic:	Tie a string on finger, place a chair in the path

Focus on the benefits of remembering. You can do this by commenting on the benefit.

- *Thank the child for her contribution.* "Thank you for taking Rover for a walk. He is much calmer now." "I appreciate your setting the table so promptly. We can eat on time and everyone will be more pleasant." One of the goals of chores is for kids to contribute to the family. Be sure to encourage this by commenting on it.
- *Phrase comments positively rather than negatively.* Tell the child what he or she *may do* when the chore is over. "You can eat as soon as you set your place," is positive. It focuses on the benefit of the task. "You can't eat lunch until you set your place," is negative. It tells the child what *not to do.*
- *Comment on what is in it for the child.* Some children need a more tangible acknowledgment than others. With younger children this can often be stickers or stars. With older children you might choose to give tickets or tokens that can be accumulated for specific items (an ice cream cone, music, sports equipment) or privileges (choosing the dinner menu, more screen time, trip to the zoo, have a friend stay overnight).

Develop consequences for forgetting. If there is no consequence for forgetting (not doing) the chore, children may conclude that it isn't really necessary. A consequence helps to make forgetting a chore less convenient or pleasant than doing it on schedule.

- **Restate expectation.** "You are expected to do your chore yourself. Tomorrow I will not remind you. If you forget, you will need to do one of my chores to make up for the time it would take me to do your chore" (preferably a chore she does not enjoy).
- **Child does the task when you notice or remind the child.** For example, he may have to do the chore in the middle of a TV show, when talking with a friend, or as he is drifting off to sleep. The goal is to make remembering more desirable than forgetting.

If needed, you can consider ideas in the "Refusal to contribute" section below.

Poor quality work

Some kids do a poor job because they really don't know how to do a good job. Maybe you told them, but if their learning style is visual or kinesthetic, the information won't stick. Or maybe the child really doesn't want to do the task and thinks that if he or she is slow enough you will give up and do the job yourself.

Teach a standard. Develop a checklist and then ask the child to grade your work. *Note:* Be sure to make some mistakes so the child has something to find. For example, if you are teaching a standard for cleaning your room, you could leave a big wrinkle in the bed, a sock peeking out from under the bed, and the trash basket tipped and overflowing.

Distinguish between poor, okay, and excellent performance. For example, a poor birthday cake might be one that is cracked, has unfrosted areas showing through, and two candles broken. An acceptable cake might be unbroken, completely frosted with "Happy Birthday" and appropriate candles. An excellent cake might have the child's name on the cake and some theme decorations (cars, flowers, etc.). Or, you might watch the Olympic figure skaters and see if you can make a list of actions that lower a score or increase it. When the child understands the concept of levels of performance, ask him or her to list the characteristics of the three levels of quality for a task you do—like the laundry. Then ask her to create criteria for her chore. When she can create the criteria, you can have her grade herself.

Child determines what needs to be fixed and the parent does it while the child watches. Parent can use self-talk. "Hmm, I wonder what is causing the wrinkle. It could be the blanket, a sheet, or something left in the bed. I'll try the blanket first."

Parent asks the child to critique the child's own job and repair omissions. "Okay, Buddy, what is good and what needs fixing?" If the child replies that the toys are put away but the bed has some wrinkles, you could say, "Right you are. When you have removed the wrinkle, call me and we will check again."

When the wrinkles are gone, you could praise him, "Wow, you had trouble getting the wrinkles out of your bedspread. You kept at it until they were gone. Congratulations on a job well done. Eventually you will be able to make your bed wrinkle-free easily." This message conveys that you will support him until he learns to do the whole job well.

We have looked at several ways to convey a standard and the idea that doing a poor job will take longer than doing a good job because you have to come back and fix the poor job.

Refusal to contribute

What will you do if your child continues to "forget" or refuses?
- *Identify the reason for resistance.* Some kids resist chores for a reason. When you identify the reason, you can problem solve a way around the issue so the task is more tolerable.
- *Introduce positive self-talk.* Some examples might be: "I can figure out a way to make this fun." "This will only take a couple of minutes if I am fast." Or, "The sooner I get started, the sooner I'll be done."
- *Child pays the person who did her chores.* The payment can be in alternate service (doing a chore for the helper) or some other compensation for the effort.
- *Family services stop.* When a child complains she doesn't have any clean socks for soccer, parent can respond, "You didn't put them in the dirty clothes. I figured you didn't want them washed."

- *Perks disappear.* Perks are a benefit of contributing to the family. They are not guaranteed. It boils down to "No work, no pay (treats or services)" Or, put another way, "If you want cooperation, you must give cooperation." Some perks might be: a ride to a friend's house or the mall, a new "thing," a favorite snack item, screen time.
- *Renegotiation.* If a child does not want to do his chore, find out what he is willing to do instead. Perhaps instead of cleaning up after dinner, the child might be willing to clean the bathroom or entertain a younger sibling so the parent has some free time.
- *Seek outside help.* There are some children who, for whatever reason, do not respond to traditional approaches. If you are working with one of these children, you might wish to seek professional advice.

When kids refuse to do chores or do them poorly some parents are tempted to link chores to money, hoping to get more cooperation. We will look at tying chores to an allowance in the next chapter.

CHAPTER 5: Tie chores to allowances?

Some parents wonder whether they should give an allowance based on the child's willingness to do chores. To answer this we will delve briefly into the topic of allowances, and then look at a balanced approach to allowances and chores.

Purpose of allowances

Most allowances serve two functions—(1) to give the child spending money, and (2) to teach money management skills.

The dole system. With the dole system, children are given money as the parents see fit. Money is not earned. Parents can give or withhold money as they wish.

The advantage of the dole system for children is they can get expensive items if they can justify the expense or if they time their requests well. The disadvantages are that children do not learn to budget or plan expenses and they may equate purchases with love and approval or as payment for staying out of the way.

Earned money system. Children can earn spending money by doing specific jobs. As children grow older, the tasks become more complex and the payment increases.

The advantage for children of the earned money system is that they have access to money. They learn to associate money with work and learn to work for the money they want. The disadvantages are that children often decide that everything has a price. Further, many children stop doing household jobs when outside jobs (babysitting, delivering newspapers, mowing lawns, etc.) bring in more money.

Family contribution system. With the family contribution system, children receive an allowance because they are family members. No additional money is given out. Money is not connected to work.

The advantage to children is they get a specific amount of money regularly. They can plan how to spend it. Money does not become a "love" issue. A disadvantage is that allowances are rarely large enough to buy the "real things" that children want. Saving for purchases often fails and children spend the money "foolishly."

Gifts. Some children receive sizable monetary gifts for birthday, holidays, and special occasions. Many of these come without restrictions.

The advantage of the gifts for children is that they can buy whatever they want, including big items. The disadvantage for most children is that the money is irregular and spent relatively quickly.

Impact of money on chores

Let us revisit the benefits of chores and see how tying chores to money might affect them.

Learning life skills. Paying for chores may speed the process of learning the skills for some children. It might also encourage the idea that every job has its price.

Understanding the reciprocal nature of life. Paying for chores would undermine the notion of giving to the common good without the expectation of personal benefit.

Self-motivation. Paying for chores would decrease self-motivation. Children would learn to rely on others to provide an incentive.

A balanced approach

Your decision will depend on your values. Each person will rank the advantages and disadvantages above differently.

A balanced approach to money and chores might be to require routine contributions (jobs) and provide a basic allowance simply for being a family member. Additional money could be earned by doing optional chores. That way children would learn there are certain responsibilities that go with being a family or group member, and also that additional effort can bring additional rewards. A challenge for many parents will be to remember to keep the routine chores separate from financial incentives or penalties.

CHAPTER **6**: Changing as kids grow

Levels of support

As your child grows it is helpful to change your level of support.

Parent as nurturer does the chore with the child and describes what he or she is doing.

Parent as teacher offers a child choices. As the child becomes more skillful making decisions, parents can offer three and then more ideas.

Parent as coach provides structure without offering choices. The parent reminds the child that she can resolve the situation without resorting to telling her what to do.

Parent as consultant offers assistance if asked. As a consultant the parent is a resource only, which the child is free to accept or not.

Chart 4: Responding with different levels of support	
Level of support	**Picking up toys**
Nurturer Does the thinking and most of the work	Works beside the child putting things away. She describes what she does. *"Let's clean this mess. First, we'll put the blocks in the box. Next we'll put the books on the bookshelf."*

continued on page 29

continued from page 28

Teacher Offers choices and maybe helps work	Asks the child what she would like to pick up next. *"Do you want to put away the puppets or the dolls now?"*
Coach Reminds the child she has the skills needed to do the chore	Asks the child to create a structure for doing the chore. *"When are you going to start putting things away?"* *"What did you do last time?"*
Consultant Acts as a resource IF the child asks	Reminds the child she is available as a resource. *"Wow! Cleaning this is going to take thought. If you get stuck, you can ask me for ideas."*

The level of support depends more on the child's experience than on his age. If a 10-year-old has never put the toys away before, you will need to start him on the nurture level and teach him what to do. However, he will take much less time to understand and move on than a toddler will.

Vary the jobs

When children are young keep the chores the same so they can master them. As children grow and can do different chores, it is often helpful to change their chores. Rotating chores will help reduce boredom and solidify skills. This is Angela's experience:

> *Angela had three children, 13, 11 and 7. One Saturday morning she received a phone call that guests, who were expected Sunday, were arriving in four hours. She called Josh, her older son, and told him to clean the bathroom. He complained, "Why do I always have to clean the bathroom?"*
>
> *Wishing to bolster his self-esteem Angela promptly answered, "Because you do such a good job." Josh replied, "You mean if I didn't do such a good job, I wouldn't have to clean the bathroom?" Mom thought a moment and replied, "Please clean the bathroom now, and when the company leaves we will talk about revising the chores."*

Angela realized that she wanted all her children to be able to clean the bathroom but she had unconsciously adopted the easy path by requiring her older son to do it.

Growing a chore as the child grows

In the beginning of the book (chart 1, page 8) we saw how you can modify the job of cleaning the bathroom as a child grows. In this section the chart illustrates how you can sequence the skills kids need to fix food, and change the job (or privilege) as kids grow.

When fixing food, as with most other tasks, children need to be supervised until they have mastered the skills for each level. The ability of any child depends on several things, among them the child's interest and ability to focus, his coordination and strength, and his experience and training. When kids don't start fixing food until elementary age, they will need to learn the basics (previous steps) before preparing food as their more experienced peers can do.

Chart 5: How a chore can grow with a child fixing food				
Stages of food preparation *See note below*	**Toddler** **1-3 yrs**	**Preschooler** **4-5 yrs**	**Elementary school**	
			6-8 yrs	**9-11 yrs**
1. Observe, shred, snap— • Watch/help the cook prepare food • Shred lettuce, snap beans	with help	alone	alone	alone
2. Spread, stir, & dump • Nothing sharp, nothing hot • Peanut butter on celery, cheese and crackers, and stirring batter	with help	coaching	alone	alone
3. Measure, pour, & microwave • Use rice cooker, toaster oven, pour beverage, cut with a butter knife, • Rice with toppings, nachos, pizza, muffins, and mixing juice	—	with help	coaching	alone
4. Chop, skewer, simple stove top • Cut with appropriate kitchen knife, use large heavy (stable) pots • Make pancakes, scramble eggs, assemble kabob, make tuna salad	—	—	with help	alone
5. Stove top, oven, follow recipes • Boil water for pasta, cook oatmeal • Fry an egg or hamburger for spaghetti; mix, shape, & bake cookies	—	—	—	with help

Note: These steps provide a reasonable sequence of experiences to offer children. The ages suggested are approximate and the children will need supervision until the grown-up in charge is confident the child can and will act safely.

Closing

Congratulations! You finished *Children and Chores: The Surprising Impact of Chores on Kids' Futures.* That took both time and effort—the two elements that can help you involve kids in chores and raise successful young adults.

We have looked at why chores are important and what you can expect at different ages. We looked at how to introduce chores and how to deal with resistence. And we looked at how to modify chores as the child grows and at the influence of money on the positive impact of chores.

Many people underestimate the ability of toddlers and preschoolers to learn practical skills. When you talked to your baby before she could talk to you, you were building her language skills. Similarly, when involving her with the chores *before* she has the skills, you are providing her with information she will need to be competent later.

I invite you to dive in and start chores at whatever age your child is. With persistent and changing support, toddlers to teens can learn to contribute to both their family and the community.

By investing time and energy now, while your child is young, you can increase the chances of rearing a successful young adult. If your child is older—even a teen—there's no time like the present to get started.

Enjoy the fruits of your efforts far into the future!

Resources

Age-Appropriate Chores. *www.familyroi.org*

Am I Doing Too Much for My Child? by Elizabeth Crary. Introduces four levels of support (or parenting) for toddlers through teens and shows how to use them for different situations and at different ages. Seattle: Parenting Press, 2011.

"Chore Wars: Researcher Finds that Involving Young Children in Household Chores Pays Off Later." Originally written by Liz Wolf for the March 2003 issue of Minnesota Parent. *http://nfb.org/legacy/fr/fr14/fr04se09.htm*

How Much Is Enough?: Everything You Need to Know to Steer Clear of Overindulgence and Raise Likeable, Responsible and Respectful Children from Toddlers to Teens by Jean Illsley Clarke, Ph.D., Connie Dawson, Ph.D., David Bredehoft, Ph.D. Clarifies the line between enough, abundance, and overindulgence. New York: Marlowe & Company, 2004.

Kids and Chores. Qwik Sheet from Parenting Press. *www.ParentingPress.com*

Love & Limits: Guidance Tools for Creative Parenting by Elizabeth Crary. Provides a short, simple, easy-to-read introduction to the STAR Parenting process, points, and tools. Seattle: Parenting Press, 1994.

Pick Up Your Socks . . . and Other Skills Growing Children Need! by Elizabeth Crary. Presents information helpful in raising a capable, responsible child. Includes a household job chart to explain when kids do selected tasks. Seattle: Parenting Press, 1990.

STAR Parenting Tales and Tools: Respectful Guidance Strategies to Increase Parenting Effectiveness & Enjoyment by Elizabeth Crary. Seattle: Parenting Press, 2011. Offers an innovative and effective process to resolve everyday parenting challenges, with lots of examples of parents using the tools.

Temperament Tools: Working with Your Child's Inborn Traits by Helen Neville and Diane Clark Johnson. Describes eight clusters of traits and how to deal with them in young children. Seattle: Parenting Press, 1998.

Understanding Temperament: Strategies for Creating Family Harmony by Lyndall Shick, M.A. Helps parents identify children's temperament and teach skills children will need to live cooperatively in the family and world outside the home. Seattle: Parenting Press, 1998.

Without Spanking or Spoiling: A Practical Approach to Toddler and Preschool Guidance by Elizabeth Crary. Introduces the basic concepts of child guidance. Seattle: Parenting Press, 1979. Revised 1993.